S0-AIY-111

The Ruins of Providence

ALSO BY KEITH WALDROP

A Windmill Near Calvary (University of Michigan Press, 1968)
Songs From the Decline of the West (Perishable Press, 1970)
The Garden of Effort (Burning Deck, 1975)
Wind Scales (Treacle Press, 1976)
Windfall Losses (Pourboire Press, 1976)
The Space of Half an Hour (Burning Deck, 1983)
The Quest for Mount Misery (Turkey Press, 1983)

THE RUINS OF PROVIDENCE

local pieces

by

Keith Waldrop

Copper Beech Press

Some of these pieces were first published in *College English, Grosseteste Review, Loose Art, Open Places, PN Review,* and *Poetry* ("Around the Block" and "Lullaby in January," copyright 1979 by the Modern Poetry Association); in *Pourboire 16: Peter Kaplan's Book;* and in *Intervals,* an Awede Press chapbook.

The publication of this book was made possible by grants from the Rhode Island State Council on the Arts and the National Endowment for the Arts, a Federal agency, in Washington, D.C.

Cover: "The Crucifixion with the Two Thieves" by the Master of the Providence Crucifixion (Utrecht, circa 1450-1460). Reproduced by permission of the Museum of Art, Rhode Island School of Design, Providence.

Copyright© 1983 by Keith Waldrop
All rights reserved.
For information, address the publisher:
            Copper Beech Press
            Box 1852
            Brown University
            Providence, Rhode Island 02912

Library of Congress Cataloging in Publication Data
Waldrop, Keith.
    The ruins of Providence.

    I. Title.
PS3573.A423R8   1983   811'.54   83-15119
ISBN 0-914278-41-X

First Edition
Printed in the United States of America

for Q.

CONTENTS

So a person having neither home nor country can still experience the characteristic stirrings of love for these things, even when they lack an object and persist therefore as yearnings without fulfilment. — Max Scheler

AROUND THE BLOCK

I will go for a walk before
bed, a little stroll to settle
the day's upsets. One thing always
follows another, but
discretely — tree after
telephone pole, for instance, or
this series of unlit houses. One moment follows
another,
helplessly, losing its
place instantly to the next. Each frame
fails, leaving behind
an impression of motion.

As for death, at the moment I
think it strangely overrated.

Who now could build
houses like these? who
could afford to? They loom
in the evening of the
East Side, memory-traces
of sometime wealth. Dust
seems forever settling, but
must somehow recirculate.

Once around the block
will do. Porch after porch projects
its columns, seeming one dark and
continuous dwelling. And fear continues,
eternal night shuttering each
source of light. How
remarkable, how remarkably
pleasant, not to be
asleep, still discriminating
dips in the sidewalk, reading
the differences between shadows.

A CEREMONY IN WOODS HOLE

for Peter Kaplan (1957-1977)

The light over the bay
is too bright to look at, and too
clear to be seen. Our tears
remain opaque, index
of unknown values.

Daylight is busy with
the surface of the sea, as that surface
engages the body of
air above it. Smoke will hover, a
while, over a dead flame.

Peter, I would rather this were
lines etched into a delicate design
representing, for instance, whales at play.
A body, lifted out of the water at Newport,
we carry past the Fishmonger to scatter it
on closer waters.

CHROMATIC STUDY

for Heide Ziegler

*.... a modulation has occurred which escaped my
comprehension.* — *Schoenberg*

From here to
you is the shortest distance,
warped over silly
surfaces proper
to a modern universe.

Between one action and another,
there is an empty time, un-
fillable. It's easy enough to
throw oneself against
an adequate breakfast or
carry a dreadful secret even
unto death, but
mile after mile of mere
motion
stretches between decisions.

"Listening to a concert," he
continues, "I often find myself,
unexpectedly,
in a foreign country."

Themes float up, in
conversation, that I
at some point noted
and sight now as
familiar objects on a new horizon, thus
known but unknown, recognized
as forgotten.

It takes complicated
projections to give us
ordinary area.

I would like to practice simple
bi-location.

In the Sea of Darkness, a
continent sinks, in *terrible con-*
vulsions. With every
expedition, islands
remove, withdrawing always
to remoter
latitudes, just beyond our
last advance.

Immeasurable, the
ocean of harmony, washing
scraps of tune onto
one or another shore, sloshing in
time, *appoggiatura*
across the Dolphin's
Ridge, each ripple
lost in
long resolves, dissonant
concord of surprising
distances, intervals at
extremes. In the midst
of spray, phantom solids.

Some would
attribute to decisions in eternity
the disorders of time.

Fire and gravel. Anything
might happen.

On an old chart of the New
World, off
the coast by Newport or,

perhaps, Japan, a bearded
Elemental gazes at the great
shell in his hands and
considers — like Wagner in
Würzburg — the fearful sounds he
will make but has
not yet made.

By the turn of thought in which
cause and effect
are rules in a geometry, our
progress falls against the
brightness of the day or
darkness of the night
sky.

Raised tones continue upward and
lowered tones drift down — part
of an attempt, merely,
to extend movement towards
the boundless and
"reconcile us to
life in general."

This pistol, like
any other, will
shoot only
into the future.

It's not troubling to me to
think the world to its
end, but I'm
deeply disturbed at
the edge of a map.

The sense of
clothes
grows on one,
nakedness
dropping away like a too
rich accumulation

which must be parceled out
in layers of
cotton, wool,
synthetic fibers,

so that, by intricate
courses, we
weave
the living with the
simple — tense
denim,
figured stuff.

"DER TOD, DAS IST DIE KÜHLE NACHT"

Even in dreams I hear
nothing but songs of passion
sung by a cardinal
from a sycamore behind the house.

Afternoon frazzled me. It's getting
dark now and I'm already half asleep.
Life has been a hot and humid
day. Death is cool night.

DRIFT

There are no
two alike. This is what they
have in common. It is
what they have in
common with all things: every separate atom
of hydrogen, say, or
oxygen, must be itself — must be
different. Blown in-
differently, they fall, they
pack, pile, fuse or refreeze, as
these particular days
drift into a winter.

With a few extra lines, the face
is lost.

Hardly anyone appreciates,
anymore, the value of secrecy.

Coming-into-being is no problem when
the desire of the eyes turns
splotches and stains any-old-how into
objects of fear, love, loathing.

Are they ours?

Two dots in a circle express,
generally speaking, enough personality.

Housetops, loaded with incoming
messages, translate them endlessly
to lower stories.

On earth's rim, but well inside the
heavens, no doubt I overestimate
the upright.

Precious puzzles, dreams, aspects of
motion, my kooky
doctrines — oh please
stay out of sight, like unpainted
parts of the
set, hidden supports to an effort
towards
just enough imagery.

Expression may be effected
without a slightest movement of any
facial muscle. A thought may be
forced out through the hands, for
example. See how nervous, then, these
fingers are.

Dangers I have not faced — dangers
of depth — are reflected on high,
warnings against too facile flight.
See, on this middle ground, whole
fleets of unlaunched craft, decaying.

Or the word "passage" in the phrase *the
passage of time* — philosophers
debate its meaningfulness. For some,
there is only time, no passage. And
for others, of course, no time either.

See how the unseen sun, behind
that solid grey sky, obscures
the decline of the afternoon.

1
Gradually to compose
you, I think against my
thought, freezing in its

flight an
idea of praise. It will

bear you out, I
hope. Also, I would like
to imitate, but

perfectly, the pitch
of quiet nights.

2
Silence in heaven strikes
common tones. Between
you and me,

one pinpoint of light is
much like another, never

mind the years that
divide them. They do
nothing to establish

the coordinates of
our walk.

3
When once the earth is
gone, God will separate
light from heat,

reserving
the heat for those in hell

and for his saints the
cold light of
love eternal. Within otherwise

"normal" scales, we
are allowed shades.

4
I disorganize my
lines to realize
your tempo. Trapped

in survival mechanisms, I
shift continually the order

of what might happen — events
change character with
each pull towards

unison. Where nothing is
noted, we rest.

5

What is your relation to
my fault? I see your
left on my right, although

we move in concert. Below the surface
great cypresses are submerged, until

one may canoe among
the branches — new lakes, waterfalls
on the level, crevices of unmeasured

depth. Are we anchored in
ordinary questions and answers?

6
It is not as if
we ever chose this
tune. Disease

runs within the
wood, damaging

perfect outlines. To
exalt a valley, some
mountain will be debased. I

step unevenly,
between terminals.

7
Our shadow
strains, as if to be
off on its own — grasps, an instant,

each tree we pass. How
much of

us is in-
volved in its
tumbling

shape? There are leaps,
unpredicted intervals.

8
Pauses consolidate a
rhythm one
might, rushing, mis-

place. "Sureness"
is not the same as

"knowing". I appreciate a tissue
like *to be,* a
certainty like

the waves against Lapland,
a cadenza like ruins.

9
Before I go, let us
put our horseplay in order. This
trope (or

conversion) will
serve its turn. Tonic to

tonic, but what
possibilities of divergence
between

here
and here.

10
A map of expected intensities will
disregard fallen and
splintered

trunks. We follow
the grain, not seeking

to make statues laugh or
dogs sing. We do not
avert our eyes or fear

a second, more hazardous,
glance. Are we near the focus?

11
Every spirit is
winged, angel and
demon alike, and may be

transfigured merely, never made
happy. I muddy

clear ideas, hurrying
to the surface. Physical
harmonies are

at our disposal, simultaneously
theatre and thought.

12
Days lose their full
emptiness if we
forget to

measure them. Above profound
features, lines on water connect

continents. Voices
unite
in the silence after

the score. It happens
and it is over.

IN THE SHADE

Echoes of a brilliant red
struggle for separation.

I walk through the shadow.

If I allow a loss
of definition,
it is ground maintained.

Whatever you are,
you are not
to be believed.

One wall holds a map
of the heavens, across from it
a view of Danzig.

This is the rainbow
of a bone.

You are at least a second
person.

If the bottom drops
out, it is
a further step.

Pronouncements, reasonable and
silly, peel
from the wall.

Light on the river
reveals a line of houses.

I never confuse darkness.

A little color
heightens
the sense of death.

"Skin-deep," you say,
and I am hoping
you mean *infinite.*

For every tone, there is a corresponding fear.

LULLABY IN JANUARY

for Elsie Michie

Bravely (it seems to me) you
close your eyes, as if never doubting
that the world remains
visible, even though you yourself see now
only side-effects of sight.

What you can't see is that it has
begun to snow, hard, as if to fulfill
a prophecy of *fatal winter* and its *fierce foul
frost.* But we have this enclosure, a space
set apart from the inhuman cold outside.

It always amazes me, how much
sleep you need, and get. And with what
ease sleep takes you, evening out your
breathing as in the most spiritual
exercises.

Just past midnight, I'm securely
awake, the hour of my birth arriving
with a wicked downdraft. These rooms, at not
quite room temperature, support a thought of green
lawn, croquet parties, seasons gradually

turning the house around. We wait
for it to happen. And it seems to me that
anyone who sleeps sleeps heroically, trusts
unreasonably that something will
come again, out of nothing.

PLANNED CITY

We travel, but not like
former travelers: trunks
heavy with a solid six
months of all necessary
effects,
clothes for the evening and for the morning.

Voyagers of the
"visitable past," they steamed across
continents and their
trunks attended them--headed always
towards the Season,
surrounded by porters bearing
their milieu.

I find it harder and harder
to start (poems, for
instance) each time afresh, from
nothing. A larger structure, however
specious, helps keep me going.

Meanwhile, wolves are in the
streets and indeed this street
belongs to the wolves. What happens
happens.

A hero, faced with a
monster in his path, refused
battle with any mere envoy. "I will fight
only," he said, "with
the god who has sent you."

Mistake:
*this was not a messenger
of the deity; it was
the deity himself.*

I would like to deny that from
here to here is always the same
distance. My mother used to
send me a card every
Mother's Day.

How is it that how-
ever we separate ourselves, sever
connections, pain still
throbs in lopped
parts, hurts us
in worlds we
think we've let go of?

Tops of mountains, with which I
am not, of
course, familiar, are suitable as
sites for shrines. Great gods
protect peaks.

Now when I think, I
think boundary stones,
against a
background of bright
wallpaper or the Palace
of the Doge. The film is
sensitive enough, but
there is an empty area no
camera can take in.

The density of the
universe, if that
sort of thing interests you:
one atom of hydrogen to two and a half
gallons of nothing.

If this city, and this
city alone (it is such a
small thing to ask — surely
to Universal Cause-and-Effect an
infraction beneath notice) *if only*
this single city might
escape...

No:
there shall not be left here one
board nailed to another.

Beetles will inherit
these sidewalks, winners
with wingcases.

The earliest pattern of a planned city, the gridiron scheme,
found in Mesopotamia, in Mohenjo-Daro, in Kyoto and Emporia,
Kansas, and which Ikhnaton followed in building his capital, is a
calculated slight to infinity, planting under the endless circle of
sky a momentary square.

The basest suburbs sparkle.

And eventually, Heather (by the
way, I
like your poems), all these
odds and ends will
begin to fit together and even,
probably, seem too obvious. It happens all
the time.

At birth whole
areas of the globe are
still uncommitted.
Something I just
picked up along
the way. My inertia,
well, my
inertia — I can
blame it on the constellations, can't I?
The pity is, in
"middle" life, I'm getting
clumsy, mis-
calculating, now,
distances between my physical
influence and
various things, some of them
breakable. And I used to
slip by so carefully, skirting
an ambush of objects poised to fall, the
planet that presided
at my birth having been
in, oh, fastidious conjunction, but now —
this on high authority — losing
its grip, wandering (taking myself
as point of reference), and from now on
whatever controls there
are for my headlong
career must proceed directly
from the stars of the microcosm.

RANGE

... the endless street, the street that stretches beyond
the range of the eye...
— Giedion, Space, Time and Architecture

Elmgrove Avenue disappears, not
in darkness or
mist — which, Lord knows, there's
plenty of in Providence — but simply
because in eight or ten blocks it
curves. Of course, if I
turn around, this end (my
end) of the street is
clear. On that corner over there,
Lovecraft was born in his
grandparents' house, long
gone, facing Angell.

Elmgrove's
no Bismarckstrasse, nothing
to compare with Broad-
way or State Street, let alone a
thirty-mile stretch in Los
Angeles. The boulevards of
Baron Haussmann are some of them
longer — all wider, more haunted.

But I cannot see to the other end
of Elmgrove, to Swan Point
Cemetery with its late
Victorian angels (you see, I
know they're there) and Lovecraft's
grave and many more elaborate
markers, bearing their inscriptions Lord
knows where, beyond all memory.

THE RUINS OF PROVIDENCE

Two oaks — in the afternoon, if
the sun is shining — cast their
shadows across Elmgrove
Avenue. Whether or not there was ever

a grove, the elms are gone.
Gone, too, in Kansas, though I
remember them luxuriant. The electric
company has hacked away

at the maple in front of my
house — chopping an airway
for their power — and it will
blaze yellow and red again this fall, but

I think it is dying. The sycamore in
back, still, sheds its bark
and shines. At least I will not
die in Kansas. Around the corner,

there are two gingko trees, fifteen
feet or so from each other — of different
sex, I suppose. It's hard to know
what to predict or even to prefer

for this terrain: oak forest like
primeval Europe, or endless gingko
grove. I love these wooden houses that
the rich built, and we live in.

SCAPE

A surface of water can be
thought of, out of all relation
to body or to

depth. Such thought
grows tense and will
support the idea of a fleet

over disregarded
layers of lost light, eyeless
undercurrents, monstrous with

suggestion. What I hear is
not always what
I have listened for.

Here, and in St. Petersburg, one
dreams of being run over by
horses in the street. St.
Petersburg, Russia, that is, at the
turn of the century. Since the Revolution,
they are more and more (horses, I
mean) a thing of the past — or of
westerns. Which brings me
to Italy, where a torrent of traffic
rushes, honking, over
the Roman Empire. But here,
and through a desert, anytime, the Nile
flows like a dream.

THE MASTER
OF THE PROVIDENCE CRUCIFIXION

for Jack & Sophie Hawkes

*Furthermore no cast shadows are found in any of
the pictures of the shop in which the Providence
panel was painted, with the odd exception of a
shadow cast by a bone...*
—David G. Carter, "The Providence Crucifixion"

*One chap had his leg blown off from standing on
a bomb. Later, in hospital, he told me that he felt
satisfied. He had always wondered what would
happen if a man stood on a bomb.*
—A. John Gallishaw, "Gallipoli"

world haunts back of mind like lens
—Bernadette Mayer, ceremony latin

Little is known concerning the extinction of images. Climbing,
as he often has to, the walk that leads steeply to the East Side
from the river, behind which rises Down Town, he ponders life
among the missing. At one time he was convinced — had convinced
himself — that he could visit, unaffected, the realm of the dead (a
result, no doubt, of wide but undisciplined reading) and this held
out to him the hope of subliming his most pedestrian fears — to
pass, as he put it, from this terrible world to a world of pure terror.

What would there be, without instigation, without the
interruptions of perception and inner need, without the unlike-
ness of dreams? If all problems, that is, were gone, what would
his fantasy be? He has heard that many men want nothing more
than to be transparent — has heard and finds it hard to accept.
There is a storm, but it is somewhere out at sea. Not our
sea — not, I mean, over the sound that stretches into the
Atlantic. And not in the Atlantic either. Hurricanes do come that
way, but this storm is elsewhere. The violence of the storm is
such that waves are thrust up in wedges of tremendous height
and weight, a surface broken within great gashes. A maelstrom
should plunge desperately down, but this one surges rather,
whirling into the upper elements.

It is *too intense* a storm. Water could not spiral so or hold such furious patterns. Some other atmosphere rages, perhaps over molten rock or exploding helium. Knowledge is not what he is after, not really. He seeks cadence.

His faculty for inner speech is, by far, too well developed. By the time he has finished talking to himself, there is almost never anything left to say. Now he is asking himself, paused, leaning slightly against the handrail — but at an angle more acute to the handrailed sidewalk — how he can have lost what he never had. Here is the question he means: how is it, when he thought himself without expectations, he finds himself so disappointed? He lives in a space severely limited, and has a tendency to deny any other space. Still, if there were another place — *some place he could know nothing of* — he would wish it well, though at a loss for any more specific benediction.

There have been people flayed alive, murdered by loved ones, dragged through a living death. Eventually their pain is effective only in the best told tales. His skull is in place. As for his thoughts, they are a forlorn hope, fully engaged still, and yet already given up for lost. Their common mission, which has sent them in preposterous directions — each along an insufficiently marked way, all out of contact — has no aura of heroism, but its perils are such that few will return. It is well known that gardens improve with age.

Nothing is more remote from his thought than the processes which make it possible. They can, of course, be thought about, mapped, turned into figures, but remain, for all that, alien. He would like to finish with a lament, for while it is appropriate to condemn many things and to commend some few, all things are lamentable. He repeats this to himself, desiring no unfilled gaps, in a mixture of fantasy and Dutch.

The way of the observer is hard. Like Job in his first anguish, he would cry that if he had not been born, *now should I have lain still and been quiet, I should have slept*. But what a remarkable sense, he thinks, of the word *sleep*: not to lose, merely, but never to have had any consciousness at all. And what a weird sense of the word *I*.

In this, as in so much, he faces two ways at once, abstracting from the most precise materials. The Burnside house is on his left, as he turns the corner left. An open space, forming the heart of the square in which the church stands, separates the solitary western tower from the choir and transept, the nave having been blown down by a violent wind and never rebuilt. So long to that close association. If I were with him, my account could *hardly be different*. My head.

What is there, as he proceeds, for him to do? He could be more exact, focus more sharply on ends and odds that proliferate along his path. But that would mean, not necessarily choosing a trail, but at least moving in one direction at a time. Whereas, when he thinks of anything in the world, some part of him regards it as treachery, like signaling — albeit without a code they could be expected to interpret — to a foreign power, potentially hostile. Though he moves on, blindly right, mistaking no turn, in a territory familiar as blinking, he is, as so often, beside himself. Still, he knows, without deliberation, how to get across Providence. It is only thought he is lost in.

Sensations — of brick under his feet, of new green around him — have a tendency to rush into him pell-mell, vanishing into a point of general well-being or malaise. It is this headlong rush, past his troubled but inefficient local soul, towards the accommodation of a warm and indefinite interior, that he distrusts. He would like to keep things at a distance, within his senses, so as to keep them present.

He is passing the Museum of Art and chooses to remember, specifically, an acquisition of the most celebrated of sufferings, with a veritable rain of blood and, in the background, Jerusalem in agony, its flaming skyline in the image of Utrecht in the fifteenth century. He wonders if those buildings were in fact destroyed by fire, or more slowly, by other agents. It is hard to care about what happens, *just because it has happened*. That is why dream images fade so fast and why a common-place, dredged from the remote past or the lower brain, is so precious.

The Crucified is certainly not comely and nothing natural commiserates — no earthquake, no eclipse, no rocks rent asunder. The horizon is high over this Jerusalem-of-the-North, so little sky apparent that only those in mortal pain reach it. Presumably it is a corpse (spear-tested already, sorrow and love) that hangs there now, two dimensional, contaminating time with eternity. The artist, too, has entered the realm of the unknown, indexed by the name of a city not yet imagined, one which has not preserved the hearts of the German emperors and does not lie against the Crooked Rhine.

He has tried often to figure out — a project that would be more sensible to pursue with some kind of measurement, but he is not sure what kind — where the center is, of this hill he lives on, one of seven. It is perhaps the dome, more capitol-like than that of the Capitol downtown, that crowns the Christian Science Church on Prospect. Lovecraft's last dwelling has been moved bodily to within a stone's throw (no shadow from the church, however, ever falls in that direction) and Lovecraft seems now, certainly, less eccentric. Perhaps, on the other hand, the center oscillates, giving place as one looks for it, now there and now there, never here.

He is a creature of left and right, up and down, forward and backward, but is forever puzzled to think that the great cyclonic winds — which he knows turn widdershins because of the earth's eastward spin — if he could see them, by looking *up,* their long spirals would be, to him, clockwise. Out of breath again, he is reminded of two machines he built when he was very young: one failed because something in it went wrong (just what, he never figured out), the other from an original fault, because such a machine could never in this world work. Young children upset during family holidays are frequently found to be children who at birth suffered from asphyxia.

The point in time is clear, for a good many of the trees he passes have just put out their most tentative green, while the sycamore, more cautious, is still completely bare. He has the notion, without any memory of having dreamt of that particular tree, that his dreams circle the sycamore, slowly, unwinding some ensorcelment. (His fascination with dreaming has little to do with the content of his dreams, which is not usually of interest, but simply with the intimate remoteness of himself as dreamer — such an immediate distance.) At least three different trees are called *sycamore*.

What comes to his mind now, without hurt, is the toothache of an Egyptian queen. And now someone who died quite young, but by now would in any case be long dead. There must be a way to use everything — or, rather, anything. (*Everything* is too far, too much, too long.) Lord, the waste.

The sycamore of the Bible is a kind of fig tree. Into it, Zachaeus — a wee little man — climbed, the better to see his Saviour. One would assume it to be the sort of tree whose branches begin down low, almost at the ground, and spread then more or less horizontally. Picture it, therefore, as costing little Zachaeus, perhaps some dignity, but a minimum of effort. And after all, maybe he was just scrabbling for figs but, spotted by the Christ, felt it less humiliating to be taken for a religious climber.

Struck by how it rains, in eternity, neither on the just nor the unjust, he feels again an old sadness rising in him and might, as of old, give way, forget what he is weeping for but weep on, bitterly. But he holds back, unwilling to allow himself a sadness so complete while knowing nothing of its origin — for it comes, seemingly, from nowhere, gathering slowly yet with an effect of suddenness. And it occurs to him that it *can be refused*. There is, he realizes, plenty of work. Hair thins and war is analyzed. *Even I* remember vast disappointment in promises fulfilled to the letter. He, as he walks, now with little inclination, thinks backward into complications from which his present might have arisen, seeing — not in time — the light of years declining. And the sun is going down.

Weep for yourselves. The old, he has found, remember themselves old and young, their middle years voided, and that vacant time arouses in retrospect — as it did in prospect — uneasy apprehensions. The sonorities he is after — lines, colors

— are, if you like, a reparation, a substitute, a consolation, small and specific, for a universal, unimaginable loss. But not *his* loss. He came into the world, like any Job, naked. Eden was never lost to him. That time is out of his mind. And neither did *he* exist (to say "I") in his mother's womb, which was certainly neither heaven nor hell — nor earth either, which only begins at the awful advent of air. A great failing, he feels, his piling up of ideas, images, random or systematic shadows, like trying to cut wood with the shape of an ax. One good brush stroke could demolish a forest of hesitation, as it takes the plow to begin a foundation.

The soul is not, as the common image would have it, *in* the body. His soul, at any rate, goes *with* him, as companion. Together, they think apart the most inseparable things, breaking the lines they think along, leaving, as a lord might, every wall breached and every barrier in fragments. The very bricks of the street they unpattern, to consider the ground's lay, and the wall of the sky, too, they penetrate.

What English novels call a sycamore is a maple (*Acer pseudo-platanus*), with helicopter seeds, like other maples. These (the bladed seeds), if properly pulled open, in the right sticky season, will stick to a child's nose, forming a false nose —insect-like, or like a mask from the Commedia dell'Arte. Near the end of most biographies, the subject's life's work "was now complete," as if there were a plan from the beginning, a form needing only to be filled out, a kit. But my head. We might hope, without too much hope, that a life may be improvised.

There must be some sense in which one could say that he advances.

The senses are extensions, merely, of primordial imagination, unsatisfied with the ninety-and-nine, seeking the lost. Dream-objects are disguised, not because of censorship, but because disguises suggest a farther search. But dreams are from the dreamer, from the dreaming I. Whatever cannot find a place in any dream, whether already dreamt or still to come — that is the world for which he hungers, imagination be damned.

If he stopped to think of it, he would remember that he

is late, that already he has been attended, vainly, many meanwhiles. He communicates badly, however, even with himself. There is, in his thinking, a collapse of function, speaker and listener having become one, the message from-less and to-less, a pretended distance between him and him. He read a story once in which, if he got it straight, a hero disguises himself so well that he kills himself, thinking he is someone else.

From some year, any year, which he might select from a list of numbers, a figure appears, distorted by time and by the most intense suffering. The figure disappears then, and the suffering — although it remains — loses personality. He is passing the Congregational Church, its windows blind with brick of a different color. Ravenna passes his mind's eye, in a bad projection. He tries to think of reasons for a postponement of the Last Judgment. To the obscure processes which condense the light into a flickering screen of half-legible characters, no adequate return, of thanks or of contempt, can possibly be made. Providence has fewer canals than most Dutch towns. Mysticism is no stranger to these parts. He can only think in an environment which is familiar to him. As he exhausts the potentiality of the environment to stimulate his interest, he turns more readily and begins to fill out, as it were, a sketch of his mental life — an activity which palls also, his mind being (so, at least, he has always regarded it) part of his environment.

Although the sky is still light, the moon, with all its blemishes, is up. From the weather, and other indications, he knows tonight will not be Watch Night. He has, I must record, no quarrel with darkness. It is the middle of the day that needs reconstructing, but on what model, or according to whose plan? If he tries to impose the structure of his eye on what he sees, the instant success of his project shows him how he has underestimated the correlation already there, his brain being to the microcosm what to the larger scheme-of-things could only be a cold, dark sun.

There are no shadows. He knows the exercise most helpful for one who desires unselfishness: death. This is a city of some age and historic interest, especially as illustrating the growth of civil liberties, and yet he is sure that — *at least in fiction* — it should be destroyed. It is this shadowless sun, almost set, invisible somewhere along a hideously bright horizon (that he is walking away from) that hurts my head most, more than the unclouded sun at noon. Eventually there is endless amnesia, like an inescapable infancy. He likes to consider opposites, such as *being mortal* and *being dead.* Or, "Imagine us," he says to himself, "together, in the same field, strolling, hand-in-hand even. Oh, the circumstances must be identical: you are in clover, and I am in green manure." Everyone looks for a city, but streets mark out his temporal possibilities and have marked out Moses Brown's farm, making it easy for him, having ascended, to cross or, if he chooses, to wander with increasing hunger. Let us hope there is no supreme being or infinite memory-bank, that all this, and more, can safely pass away. One day's pattern interferes with the next, or with the one before. Blood, like bone, develops from the delicate ghost skeleton, and when blood runs out it is as much a loss of structure as if the harder material were drained away. Sometimes a house he is passing emits the uncanny aura of a posthumous edition signed by the author.

"Thunder and lightning," he says, under his breath, not communicating with the day, as it disappears, but invoking changes of atmosphere. He has always felt a guest in these parts and sometimes hankers to see the program ruined. "Can you tell me," he goes on, "Delaware," — addressing nobody by the proper name — "where, if it starts here, the collapse will end?" Most things, he of course realizes, are out of the question. "As if the self, impersonal, would ever say I!" A stone wall runs the block beside the sidewalk and he runs his fingertip along a line of mortar. It is not, as a gesture, important to him, but in all the world, in any world, there is nothing more objective than what he feels at that extremity — and has now, already, forgotten.

He admits that blood is life and, further, insists that in the space of the body, blood is time. From Adam clean to him there is a line of blood. How can he travel, but at the speed of time? Blood rains on all spectators.

The western rim of the sky, behind him, indicates how much life remains. As its red accumulates and deepens, so gradually the color of vegetation fades along with the aerial blue, absorbed — both — by blood-filled clouds which give back only their own violent hue. Brick streets shine then, as if belonging to sunset.

The nature of a hieroglyphic, lying across this block of frame houses, is to retain the picture, schematized, allowing the meaning a perch on which, ever so slowly, deliberately, to collect itself. He craves the body. He ruffles what he can reach of a whole species of speculation. His features return, baffled, from brickwork and crosswalks. There is always, after blood, the possibility of fire — do wooden houses not invite the thought of it?

For his part, the suggestion is always there, in the flash of daylight on facade, in a line of roof silhouetted by the moon. It having once entered his mind, there is no wall so solid that he does not see it as dense, deceptive smoke. His eyes, indeed, smart and his breath catches a moment — a reflex, to avoid choking.

He would proceed then to choke, were it not that, along with his reaction, the whole scene is — always — suspended. Houses stand, their walls planted, though heaving with the notion of combustion. It is a city, now, of smoke, a garden of lost growth, consumed and intact. To go down the hill would be to pass between ramparts of potential ash, to descend amid furnaces whose calm windows reflect his conviction of disaster.

Particularly while he sleeps, timbers blaze, surrounding him with fierce light, tepid, flickering — unburning, the essential fire. It is not the larger vessels of the brain, not the very small ones, but those of medium size, the most ordinary, that contract and send out meridians of pain and nausea. My head breaks in waves, it would seem, past enduring. The sycamore here is the plane tree, which *pseudo-platanus*, as its name suggests, impersonates. It buds late, like the linden, but grows large leaves and spreads them with panache over the summer. When, in autumn, it lets them drop, it sheds also plates of bark and stands then — the seeds are hung in balls, some of which fail to fall —with a trunk patchy as if with scales, an orange cast where the wood shows through. The limbs, however, stretch out, greenish except where bark, in meager sheets, remains. It supports long narrow ranges of snow and ice, and in spring is again cautious, letting the maples try the field first.

He goes to bed late and sleeps into the day, like a peninsula.

May our sleep be slow, and without paradox. The country round about is pretty and plentifully studded with country houses, especially on the road to Arnhem.